Cryp Beginners Bible

How You Can Make

Money Trading and

Investing in Cryptocurrency

Written By

Stephen Satoshi

Stephen Satoshi

☐ *Copyright 2019 by Stephen Satoshi - All rights reserved.*

The following eBook is reproduced below with the goal of providing information that is as accurate and reliable as possible. Regardless, purchasing this eBook can be seen as consent to the fact that both the publisher and the author of this book are in no way experts on the topics discussed within and that any recommendations or suggestions that are made herein are for entertainment purposes only. Professionals should be consulted as needed prior to undertaking any of the action endorsed herein.

This declaration is deemed fair and valid by both the American Bar Association and the Committee of Publishers Association and is legally binding throughout the United States.

Furthermore, the transmission, duplication or reproduction of any of the following work including specific information will be considered an illegal act irrespective of if it is done electronically or in print. This extends to creating a secondary or tertiary copy of the work or a recorded copy and is only allowed with express written consent from the Publisher. All additional right reserved.

The information in the following pages is broadly considered to be a truthful and accurate account of facts and as such any inattention, use or misuse of the information in question by the reader will render any resulting actions solely under their purview. There are no scenarios in which the publisher or the original author of this work can be in any fashion deemed liable for any hardship or damages that may befall them after undertaking information described herein.

Additionally, the information in the following pages is intended only for informational purposes and should thus be thought of as universal. As befitting its nature, it is presented without assurance regarding its prolonged validity or interim quality. Trademarks that are mentioned are done without written consent and can in no way be considered an endorsement from the trademark holder.

Financial Disclaimer:

I am not a financial advisor, this is not financial advice.

This is not an investment guide nor investment advice.

I am not recommending you buy any of the coins listed here. Any form of investment or trading is liable to lose you money. There is no single "best" investment to be made, in cryptocurrencies or otherwise. Anyone telling you so is deceiving you. There is no "surefire coin" - one again, anyone telling you so is deceiving you. With many coins, especially the smaller ones, the market is liable to the spread of misinformation. Never invest more than you are willing to lose. Cryptocurrency is not a get rich quick scheme.

"The ones who are crazy enough to think they can change the world are the ones who do". - Steve Jobs

"The stock market is a vehicle to transfer wealth from the impatient to the patient" - Warren Buffett

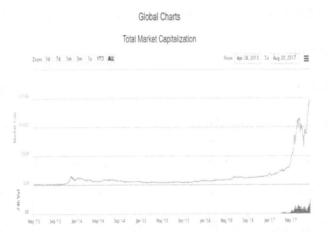

Total Cryptocurrency Market Capitalization on August 20th 2017

Source: Coinmarketcap.com

Contents

Introduction

In just 7 short years, the value of Bitcoin has increased from $0.08 to over $4000[1]

In just a single year, Ethereum's price rose from $11 to $395 and back down to $295 at the time of writing.

The current cryptocurrency market is worth around $130 billion, more than the total GDP of countries like Hungary and Kuwait.

These investment returns are completely unprecedented from any traditional stock or index fund using fiat currency - which is precisely why the cryptocurrency universe is exploding.

[1] Source: Coincap.io - 2017 price as of 22/08/2017

We have daily news articles perpetrating "Bitcoin value could reach $5000 by 2018" and yet 2 results further down on a Google search we have a contrary article with the headline "Bitcoin value has peaked says Billionaire."

In the month of July alone we saw predictions of Ethereum being at $1000 by the end of 2017, and other commentators speculating that the value would plummet to just $50 in the same time period.

It's safe to say - there's a whole lot of hype out there

This book is designed to separate fact from fiction, we want to take a step back from the hype and look at the fundamentals of some of the more prominent cryptocurrencies to examine their viability as both as technological entity and as a trading/investing vehicle. This is to give you a well rounded view on whether these coins have potential for you to make money - which many of them do

For reference purposes, I will refer mostly to Bitcoin when talking about general cryptocurrency technology and using cryptocurrency as a means of exchange. Further, in-depth explanation of Ethereum and other altcoins can be found later in the book.

Finally - if you enjoy this book, I'd really appreciate it if you took just 2 minutes of your time to leave it a review on Amazon.

What is Cryptocurrency?

Depending on who you ask, defining cryptocurrency will elicit answers from "the money of the future" all the way down to "the biggest bubble since the DOTCOM bubble". US senator Thomas Carper summed it up best in laymens terms.

"Virtual currencies, perhaps most notably Bitcoin, have captured the imagination of some, struck fear among others, and confused the heck out of the rest of us."

For a more accurate definition, cryptocurrencies are simply currencies that do not have a centralized lender like a country's central bank. They are created using encryption techniques that limit the amount of monetary units (or coins) created and then verify any transfer of the funds after their creation.

This creation technique is known as "mining" due to its theoretical similarity to mining gold or other precious metals. To mine cryptocurrency, one needs to solve an increasingly complex computer algorithm or puzzle. Solving these algorithms takes a lot of computer processing power, and consequently, electricity. In other words, it costs money to mine them, so we can't just create value out of thin air. Therefore these currencies and their value are secured by the laws of mathematics as opposed to any central government or bank.

As cryptocurrency adoption increases, so does the number of real world uses. Everything from physical goods, gift cards, tickets to sports games and even hotel bookings can be purchased using cryptocurrency. Certain bars and restaurants have now also started accepting it as a means of payment. A number of NGOs now accept donations in Bitcoin and other cryptocurrencies as well. There are also more illicit uses, with the cases of underground online marketplaces dealing in illegal goods, such as Silk Road and AlphaBay.

These currencies have a huge number of advantages versus the currencies that we know and use today. This is what makes them so attractive to both long term investors and short term speculators. Of course, like any investment, cryptocurrencies do indeed have some potential drawbacks to them - and we will examine these later on in this book.

An Extremely Brief History of Cryptocurrency

While the practical applications of cryptocurrencies date back a mere 7 years, the technical aspects actually date back a further 30 years to the 1980s. Cryptographer David Chaum was the first to theorize a cryptocurrency when he invented an encrypted computer algorithm that allowed secure, unalterable exchanges between two parties.

Chaum later founded DigiCash, one of the first companies to produce units of currency based of his algorithm. It's important to note that only the DigiCash company, could produce the currency, which is a model unlike Bitcoin and other cryptocurrencies where anyone can mine the currency (providing they have the necessary computing power). After running into legal problems and rejecting a partnership with

Microsoft that would have seen DigiCash paired with every home Windows operating system, the company went bankrupt in the late 1990s.

Chinese software engineer Wei Dai published a white paper on "b-money", which laid the foundations for the architecture behind the cryptocurrencies that we know today. The paper included information on complex algorithms, anonymity for purchasers and decentralization. However the currency itself never came to fruition.

US based E-Gold was another failed attempt at creating a cryptocurrency in the 1990s. The Florida based company gave customers e-gold "tokens" in exchange for their jewelry, old trinkets and coins. These tokens could then be exchanged for US dollars. The website was initially successful and there were over 1 million active accounts by the mid-2000s. One E-Gold's pioneering strategies was that anyone could open an account. However, this led to a number of scams being run through the website. In addition, poor security protocols led to large hacking incidents and the company went out of business in 2009.

The modern cryptocurrencies that we know today began with Bitcoin, which was first outlined by anonymous entity (the identity has never been confirmed as a single person or group) Satoshi Nakamoto. Bitcoin was released to the public in early 2009 and a large group of enthusiasts began mining, investing in, and exchanging the currency. The first Bitcoin market was established in February 2010.

In late 2012 Hosting and website development platform Wordpress became the first major retailer to support payment in Bitcoin. This step was key as it gave the currency real world credibility and showed that large corporations had confidence in it as a currency.

Cryptocurrency vs. Traditional Currency

Currency 101: The value of any currency is determined by what someone will give you in exchange for said currency.

Currencies, crypto or otherwise need to follow three basic rules:

1. They need to be difficult to produce (cash) or find (gold or other precious metals)

2. They need have a limited supply

3. They need to be recognized by other humans as having value

Using only Bitcoin (BTC) as an example, it ticks the boxes of all three of these characteristics:

1. Bitcoin uses complex computer algorithms in its production which take a lot of computational power, so it cannot be replicated easily or at a discount

2. There are a finite supply of Bitcoins - 21 Million to be exact[2]. As of 2015, roughly 2/3 of this number had been mined

3. There are hundreds of Bitcoin exchanges and Bitcoin is accepted everywhere from Subway to online dating sites

Where cryptocurrencies differ from traditional currencies (also known as fiat currencies) is that they are not tied to any one country, nation or institution (in most cases). There are no USA bitcoins, no Japanese Litecoins or any country

---

[2] The actual supply numbers are measured in Satoshi (0.00000001BTC). There are 2,100,000,000,000,000 (2.1 quadrillion) Satoshi.

specific altcoin. This is known as decentralization.

We also have to remember that fiat currencies that we know and love were not always the main players in the currency world. For centuries, Gold and other precious metals were seen as the most desirable currencies for day to day usage. It was not until governments could standardize and verify the metallic content of coins (and later paper bills) that they became the go to choice for citizens.[3]

Bitcoin was designed as a "deflationary currency" - meaning over time its value will, in theory, inherently increase. Unlike fiat currencies which are inflationary and whose value will eventually decrease. After all, in 1917,

[3] Until rappers start rhyming about Bitcoins and Satoshis rather than Dollar Bills, Fiat will be the dominant form of currency

$1 was worth the equivalent of $20.17 today. So the US Dollar is worth 20 times LESS than 100 years ago. In other words, if you continue to hold $1 over the course of 100 years, you will be able to buy progressively fewer and fewer items in exchange for it, whereas with Bitcoin, in theory, the opposite will happen.

As another real world example. On 22 May 2010, Laszlo Hanyecz made the first real-world cryptocurrency transaction by buying two pizzas in Jacksonville, Florida for 10,000 BTC. Today 10,000 BTC is worth over $40 million.

Bitcoin was designed this way so that no single person (or government) could increase the supply of money, lowering the value of the money already in the market.

Legendary Economist John Maynard Keynes had this to say about inflation and inflationary currencies.

"By a continuing process of inflation, governments can confiscate, secretly and unobserved, an important part of the wealth of their citizens. By this method they not only confiscate, but they confiscate arbitrarily; and, while the process impoverishes many, it actually enriches some. The sight of this arbitrary rearrangement of riches strikes not only at security, but at confidence in the equity of the existing distribution of wealth."

While Bitcoin has an air of uncertainty about it, based on the decentralization principle - where the real potential lies is in seeing it from the opposite perspective. With no single body being responsible for the supply of money, it forces all players (government, businesses and consumers) to be transparent about their processes, lowering the risk of fraud or tampering. The transparency is ensured by rewarding miners for their efforts (in the form of coin). This single dominating factor is why so many investors are confident about the long term viability of the currency.

One common argument made by Bitcoin detractors is that as there is no government backing the currency, it could totally collapse in theory. However, we have seen these happen numerous times with fiat currency under scenarios of hyperinflation where governments can no longer ensure the value of their money and as such have to create an entirely new currency. Common examples include the German Weimar Republic in the 1920s, where the currency lost so much of its value, that banknotes were used as wallpaper. Currently, the Venezuelan economy is on track to experience over 1000% inflation for the year, leaving many citizens unable to afford daily necessities like bread. Bitcoin enthusiasts see the cryptocurrency as recession-proof.

The cost of international transactions is another area where cryptocurrencies maintain a huge advantage over traditional ones. Anyone who has ever had to send money overseas will know that the cost of processing these transaction can reach ridiculous levels. There are times when these fees can top 10%. As cryptocurrencies do not view international transactions (as there are no "nations" involved) any differently from local ones, there are minimal fees for sending money to any part of the world.

The speed of transactions across borders is also much faster than regular fiat currencies, a Bitcoin transaction takes around 10 minutes to register as opposed to days for international bank transfers, and other coins process transactions even faster.

Understanding Blockchain Technology

So with no central lender like a Government backed bank, how is all this money worth anything at all? This answer is blockchain technology. If you plan to invest any money at all into cryptocurrencies, it is vital that you have at least a basic understanding of blockchain technology and its uses.

Blockchain technology allows for a permanent, incorruptible record of all transactions that have ever taken place, free from human errors or data loss. The important thing to remember is that these transactions do not always have to be financial, they can be in the form of legal contracts, auditing consumer goods and file storage.

Blockchain is essentially a giant database that is not stored in a central location. A floating database if you will. Because it is not stored in any single location, transactions recorded on the blockchain are publicly accessible and verifiable. We again go back to the idea of decentralization, and not having to rely on a single person or government to ensure our transactions will be safe.

In more practical terms, imagine all your financial information was stored on a single spreadsheet, not particularly safe right? Even if you had online and offline backups, these would be just 2 or 3 points of failure. What blockchain allows for is that spreadsheet to be shared across thousands of databases and continuously refreshed meaning that any changes would be recorded and no hacker could corrupt it at a single point of entry. As there is no single point of entry, there is now no single point of failure either.

Blockchain technology could be used to transfer everything from cryptocurrency, to tangible assets such as property without having to use a middle man such as a bank or other financial institution. This has potential to save consumers and businesses billions of dollars a year that are spent on transaction fees. While Bitcoin has gathered more mainstream press with regards to consumers, blockchain technology receives more interest from businesses.

How does Blockchain relate to Bitcoin and Cryptocurrency?

Bitcoin is not blockchain and blockchain is not Bitcoin or any other cryptocurrency. Bitcoins or other cryptocurrencies are transacted over a public network that runs on blockchain technology.

Blockchain is the underlying technology that allows bitcoin and other cryptocurrency transactions, but as previously mentioned - blockchain technology has many more potential uses. You can think of blockchain as an operating system, and Bitcoin as one of the hundreds of applications that run on that system.

Bitcoin and Cryptocurrency Drawbacks

Lack of Financial Regulation and The Ability to Fund Black Market Activity

One of the biggest strengths of cryptocurrencies is also a weakness in the system. The anonymity they provide allows them to be used to facilitate large scale black market operations and their usage for purposes of money laundering. For example, Silk Road - an underground dark net marketplace acted as a black market for illegal drugs. Payments were made in Bitcoin to protect the anonymity of buyers and sellers. The site was shut down in 2013 after amassing roughly $1.2billion in revenue. Founder Ross William Ulbricht was convicted of 8 charges and sentenced to life in prison.

Another nefarious use of cryptocurrency is in ransomware. Ransomware refers to malicious software that hackers install on a user's computer, then demand payment in Bitcoin to unscramble the software and allow the victim to access their data again. Ransomware schemes gained in popularity as using cryptocurrency as a means of payment means the people behind the attacks can seamlessly receive their ransom without revealing their identity.

Hackers

The elephant in the room regarding cryptocurrencies, with any early stage technology (which cryptocurrency very much is) there are bound to be breaches in security. Hackers have been responsible for some of the largest dips in the cryptocurrency market.

Tokyo based Bitcoin exchange Mt. Gox suffered losses of over $27.2 million and users lost over $460 million worth of Bitcoin after the exchange was hacked in 2011. At the time it was the largest cryptocurrency exchange on Earth. Amid talk of lazy management, and poor security protocols, the exchange ended up going bankrupt after the hacking incident.

Bitfinex, a Hong Kong based exchange was hacked in 2016 and its customers lost roughly $72 million worth of Bitcoin.

It is important to note that any hacking incidents regarding Bitcoin or other cryptocurrencies were done at the exchange or wallet level - not at the technology level. For further information on how to safely store your cryptocurrency, visit the wallets section of this book.

Data Loss and Human Error

If properly secured, cryptocurrencies will facilitate a shift away from physical cash which can degenerate and erode over time. As the data is encrypted and stored online, there is no way anyone (bar hackers) can access your funds.

However, this theory assumes perfect accountability from the user. As you may have figured out by now, none of us are perfect. We lose things. For example, we can lose our private encryption keys if they are stored on paper, or devices can become damaged or stolen if we are using physical encrypted wallets (like USB wallets).

Speculation and Misinformation

As previously mentioned, Bitcoin, and cryptocurrencies in general are a frontier technology. As such, mainstream media outlets, many of whom do not employ experts in the field, are liable to present misinformation regarding the technology, and the market itself. Blanket statements such as "bitcoin is better at being gold, than gold" do nothing but undermine the technology in the long run - but do make good soundbites for mainstream media

In June 2017, the Ethereum market briefly crashed after unsubstantiated rumors, perpetrated by 4Chan, claimed that founder Vitalik Buterin had died in a car crash. The hoax caused the market value to drop by around $4 billion in under 24 hours. This demonstrates that the volatility of the market in general is subject to manipulation by nefarious forces.

If you are planning on trading cryptocurrencies, you must be willing to experience sharp drops and rises in the market, far larger movements than traditional stocks. This is where being a rational trader will help you tremendously.

China

China's relationship with cryptocurrency is unlike any other country. No single nation has done more for the success of cryptocurrency than the Middle Kingdom itself. Cryptocurrencies are popular among Chinese investors due to the government's strict controls on their fiat currency, the Yuan. The biggest one of these being their currency devaluations, which hurt its value for trading and investing purposes.

This has led to many private individuals, both wealthy and non-wealthy, looking for alternative ways to grow their wealth. Cryptocurrencies are viewed by many as a more stable asset when compared to traditional investments. China's large quantity of cheap energy has also made it a hotbed for the cryptocurrency mining scene, which is now financially out of reach of most regular Western

European or Americans. Around 70% of the global cryptocurrency mining scene is located in China.

China is also liable for mass information manipulation. Mistranslations, rumour-mongering and coin pumps are all more susceptible in the Chinese market due to the lack of availability of foreign media - especially in the cryptocurrency space. In June 2017, the People's Bank of China (PBoC) issued a statement addressing false reports that the central bank was issuing cryptocurrency itself. The reports were thought the be part of a pyramid scheme to gain investors under the false pretense of a government backed cryptocurrency.

Survivorship Bias & Gambler's Fallacy

Contrary to what you may be seeing on internet forums & social media. There are people who have lost money in cryptocurrency. It's simply a matter of buying and selling at the wrong time.

It's the same reason casinos continue to do so well in part, the winners brag to their friends and family, while the loser stay silent.

Remember: **Never invest more than you can afford to lose**

This cartoon from XKCD sums it up perfectly.

NEVER STOP BUYING LOTTERY TICKETS, NO MATTER WHAT ANYONE TELLS YOU.

I FAILED AGAIN AND AGAIN, BUT I NEVER GAVE UP. I TOOK EXTRA JOBS AND POURED THE MONEY INTO TICKETS.

AND HERE I AM, PROOF THAT IF YOU PUT IN THE TIME, IT PAYS OFF!

EVERY INSPIRATIONAL SPEECH BY SOMEONE SUCCESSFUL SHOULD HAVE TO START WITH A DISCLAIMER ABOUT SURVIVORSHIP BIAS.

How to Buy Cryptocurrency

There are two ways to buy cryptocurrencies, the first is to use fiat currency (USD, EUR, GBP etc.) to purchase cryptocurrency via an exchange. These exchanges function the same way as regular foreign currency exchanges do. The prices fluctuate on a daily basis, and like regular currency exchange markets - they are open 24/7. These exchanges make their money from charging a small fee for each transaction.

Some charge both buyers and sellers, some only charge a fee for buying. For security reasons, most of these exchanges will require you to verify your ID before allowing you to purchase cryptocurrency.

It is also important to note the type of payments each exchange supports. Some allow for debit/credit card payments whereas other only accept paypal or bank wire transfers. Below are the three biggest and reputable currency exchanges for purchasing BitCoin, Ethereum and other altcoins with fiat currency like US dollars, Euros or British Pounds.

Coinbase

Currently largest currency exchange in the world, Coinbase allows users to buy, sell and store cryptocurrency. Coinbase is undoubtedly the most beginner friendly exchange for anyone looking to get involved in the cryptocurrency market. They currently allow trading of BitCoin, Ethereum and LiteCoin using fiat currency as a base. Known for their stellar security procedures and insurance policies regarding stored currency. The exchange also has a fully functioning iPhone and Android app for buying and selling on the go, very useful if you are looking to trade.

If you sign up for Coinbase using this link, you will receive $10 worth of free Bitcoin after your first purchase of more than $100 worth of cryptocurrency.

http://bit.ly/10dollarbtc

Kraken

Based in Canada, and currently the largest exchange in terms of volume of buys in Euros, Kraken has the advantage of more coin support (they also allow the purchase of Monero, Ethereum Classic and Dogecoin) than Coinbase. It allows margin trading, which while beyond the scope of a beginner, will be of interest to more experienced traders

For other cryptocurrencies such as Dash and Golem, you will need access to an exchange that facilitates cryptocurrency to cryptocurrency trading. The best one of these is Poloniex.

Poloniex

With more than 100 different cryptocurrencies available and data analysis for advanced traders, Poloniex is the most comphrehensive exchange on the market. Low trading fees are another plus, this is a great place to trade your Bitcoin or Ethereum into other cryptocurrencies. The big drawback of Poloniex is that it does not allow fiat currency deposits, so you will have to make your initial Bitcoin or Ethereum purchases on Coinbase or Kraken.

How to send BTC from one exchange to another

If you're interesting in buying altcoins that are available on Poloniex or other exchanges for BTC, then you will first need to deposit BTC onto one of these exchanges. To do so from your Coinbase account click the "send/request" button and follow the steps below

1. Enter the wallet address of the account you're sending it to (e.g. your Poloniex BTC wallet address)

2. Select the correct Coinbase account that you are transferring funds from (e.g. your BTC wallet)

3. Enter the amount you wish to send

Cryptocurrency Guide

Beyond Bitcoin, there are a vast number of currencies emerging. Some with different characteristics and advantages over Bitcoin itself.

In this section we will examine many different cryptocurrencies and the fundamentals behind them in order to give you the best possible concise information regarding each one. The prices of these coins range from <$1 to over $300 per coin so there's something for everyone here.

One additional note to remember, is that cryptocurrencies are divisible, unlike regular stocks. For example, you cannot buy less than 1 share of Apple stock (currency $159.30). However, you can buy fraction of a Bitcoin or other cryptocurrencies. Meaning that even if you only have a small amount of cash to invest initially, you can still partake in the market, even if you can't afford an entire coin.

It should be noted that as of August 1 2017, Bitcoin and Bitcoin Cash operate as 2 separate coins. A further in-depth discussion of Bitcoin cash can be found later on in this book.

For each coin I have tried to list all major exchanges that list the coin as a purchasable asset. However, exchanges continue to list additional coins all the time. For a full up to date list of exchanges that carry your coin visit http://coinmarketcap.com

Things to Consider Before Investing in Cryptocurrency

It's not essential to know all the technical details behind a cryptocurrency before investing. However, answering some basic questions will help you decide whether you should invest in a coin or not. Here are some comprehensive questions you should know the answer to before delving into a currency.

- What problem does the coin propose to solve?

- How will the coin solve this problem?

- Why is this coin's solution the best solution out there? Is it the best solution?

- Who is the team behind the coin? What is their development history? How transparent is their code? Is it open source?

- Is there a public figurehead who will take accountability for any issues with development or adoption?

- Does this coin have competitor coins? If so, what is coin A's advantage versus coin B?

Bitcoin (BTC)

Price at time of writing - $4,070.13

Available on:

Fiat: Coinbase, Poloniex, Kraken

The coin that started it all is now one of the world's premiere assets. Sitting at a market cap of over $67 billion, the coin is worth more than global companies such as PayPal. We've already discussed Bitcoin in depth previously, so this section will discuss it for investing purposes.

With the price now sitting at a staggering $4,000 per coin, many commentators have claimed that owning Bitcoin is out of reach for the regular investor, but that's a stance I disagree with.

First of all, we have to remember that cryptocurrencies are not like regular stocks, in that they are divisible. So if you wanted to invest in Bitcoin, you don't have to purchase an entire coin. You can buy fractions of the coin so even if you only have $100, you can still get started in the cryptocurrency market.

Secondly, Bitcoin's deflationary designed role as a form of "digital gold" continues to make it the world's most valuable cryptocurrency. It also makes Bitcoin ideal to hold as part of your portfolio as many other currencies price movements are linked to it.

Another reason why any portfolio should contain Bitcoin is that if you want to purchase some of the lesser known cryptocurrencies, you will have to do so via exchanging them for Bitcoin as opposed to buying them outright for fiat currency.

Bitcoin Cash (BCH/BCC)

Price at time of writing - $326.77

Exchanges:

Fiat: Bitfinex, Kraken, Bithumb (ROK) ViaBTC (CN), Bter (CN), Huobi (CN), Bitcoin Indonesia (INR)

BTC: Bittrex, Poloniex, Cryptopia (NZ)

Bitcoin cash emerged as the result of a split or "hard fork" in the Bitcoin technology on August 1st 2017. The end-goal of Bitcoin Cash is to function as a global currency.

The split occured out of problems with Bitcoin's ability to process transactions at a high speed. For example, the Visa network processes around 1,700 transactions per second whereas Bitcoin averages around 7. As the network continues to grow, so do waiting times for transactions. BCC aims to run more transactions, as well as, providing lower transactions fees.

One of the major solutions to this issue is increasing the size of each block, so that more data can be processed at once. This is in line with solving the problems of scalability that Bitcoin was facing previously. The technology itself is worked in the short-term, with the first

Bitcoin Cash block registering 7,000 transactions compared with Bitcoin's 2,500.

The success of failure of Bitcoin Cash will largely depend on Bitcoin's own adoption of the SegWit technology later this year, and the ability to process transactions quicker to act truly as a currency - rather than a speculative asset. Detractors have also raised security concerns about Bitcoin Cash.

Bitcoin Cash has been widely adopted by many cryptocurrency exchanges. At the time of writing, there is only a few weeks worth of data available and thus, no one has been able to execute any long-term trends or technical analysis of BCH as a commodity. As further adoption continues, the price may well continue to rise. Early price rises for Bitcoin Cash have been largely driven by demand from South Korea, with over 50% of the total trade volume being seen on South Korean exchanges.

Miners have been quick to adopt the currency as well due to its higher mining ROI when compared to Bitcoin. The decrease in mining difficulty (leading to greater rewards for mining) will continue to see for miners move their resources from Bitcoin into Bitcoin Cash.

Note: Depending on your exchange, Bitcoin Cash may use the symbol BCC or BCH - double check before executing a trade

Ethereum (ETH)

Price at time of writing - $225.07

Available on:

Nearly every major exchange will allow buying of Ethereum for both fiat currency and exchange with BTC

If Bitcoin dominated the cryptocurrency space from 2008-2016, 2017 has undoubtedly been Ethereum's year. This relatively new cryptocurrency has made an immediate impact upon the space with some incredible technological innovations that have the potential to be groundbreaking, and game changing.

It is worth noting that Ethereum itself is not a cryptocurrency, it is a blockchain based platform. However tokens denominated as "ether" are traded on various exchanges. These tokens can be used for making payments on the Ethereum blockchain or exchanged for other cryptocurrencies or fiat currency. Many online articles will use the terms "Ethereum" and "Ether" interchangeably.

Where Ethereum shines is with a revolutionary technology known as "smart contracts". Dubbed by some as a technology that could potentially replace lawyers and accountants, these contracts are programmable contracts using blockchain technology, that can be set to execute automatically once a certain set of conditions are met. For example, an automatic deposit of 10 ether could be made into person A's wallet, once person A completes a task for person B. Person B has no way of breaking this contract once the conditions are met as the blockchain will enforce the conditions of said contract.

The potential applications for smart contracts are vast. From government, to management, to being able to set up a self-executing will, this is truly remarkable technology. A number of large international banks have already set up think tanks for technology like this, and adoption by any large institution has the potential to send Ethereum's price into the stratosphere. The Blockchain Banking Consortium project involves 43 international banks and aims to create a blockchain network that can enable large scale international fund transfer.

The platform is still in the development stage, and there are to this day, few real world examples of large scale Ethereum blockchain implementation. However, many investors have faith in the technology, which plays a big part in explaining the price rises over the course of 2017. In less than 1 month between May 18 and June 12, the price soared from $96.65 to a peak of $395.03.

Ethereum also suffered from a $4 billion single day loss in market cap after a hoax rumor regarding the death of founder Vitalik Buterin gained traction after originating on internet message board 4Chan. Let this example be another warning that cryptocurrencies are more susceptible to market manipulation than traditional assets.

Ripple (XRP)

Price at Time of Writing - $0.15

Available on:

Fiat: Bitstamp, GateHub

BTC: Poloniex, Bittrex, Kraken, Coincheck (JP), Bitso (MEX), Coinone (ROK)

The third largest cryptocurrency by market capitalization is one that flies under the radar of most investors and news sources. Launched in 2012 and acting as a payment network and protocol, Ripple aims to enable "secure, near instant and nearly free global financial transactions." Ripple transactions currently process in an average of just 4 seconds. The platform's ultimate goal is to make outdated payment platforms with slow transactions times and high fees like SWIFT or Western Union obsolete.

Many global banking institutions already use Ripple's payment infrastructure, including giants like BBVA, Bank of America and UBS. For example, using Ripple's payment platform, banks could convert currencies seamlessly, even for obscure countries and currencies such as a conversion of Albanian Lek to Vietnamese Dong. This would also negate the need for intermediary currencies such as US dollars or Euros. According to Ripple themselves, a switch to the platform can save banks an average of $3.76.

With adoption in the global banking sector, Ripple is off to a strong start. Especially if you look at it like you would a traditional startup.

Ripple also has the largest number of coin tokens (known as XRP) available out of any coin at 100 billion (39 billion available to the public), in contrast Bitcoin only has 16 million and Ethereum 94 million.

Unlike many open source cryptocurrencies, Ripple's source code is privately owned. The 100 billion coin supply was also "instamined", and in theory the owners could generate more at any given time, which would instantly devalue anyone holding coins. The central ownership is also at a clash with those who believe that cryptocurrency should be used as a force against one single owner. Researchers at Purdue University also determined that the platform had "security concerns", although as of writing, there have been no major incidents with the platform.

Dash (DASH)

Price at time of writing - $194.25

Available on:

Fiat: Bitfinex, xBTCe, Bithumb (ROK),

BTC: Poloniex, Bittrex, Kraken

Short for digital cash, Dash focuses on speed of transaction and anonymity as its 2 main selling points. Previously known as Darkcoin, it was rebranded in order to distance itself from the "dark web" of underground illegal cryptocurrency activity. Dash focuses on privacy, usability and the consumer market. Currently the coin fluctuates between the 5th and 8th largest cryptocurrency by market capitalization.

By speeding up transaction speeds from Bitcoin by using its Masternode network, payments are near instant versus the 10 minute waiting period for Bitcoin transactions. To obtain a masternode, users must deposit a total of 1,000 DASH. This had led to some debate about whether DASH is truly a decentralized currency or not.

Dash is less liquid than Bitcoin, meaning you may have a harder time executing large orders. However, the currency continues to be adopted by more exchanges every month. Dash's growth potential remains determined by its level of accessibility and adoption by the mass market. Once such example of this is BitCart, an Irish based discount gift card website which offers customers up to 20% discounts on Amazon purchases for payment in Dash.

Another interesting area in which Dash is utilized is the recent Venezuelan currency crisis. Venezuelan Cryptocurrency exchange CryptoBuyer began selling Dash as an alternative to the local Bolivar currency which was, and still is, suffering from hyperinflation.

Venezuelans are seeking to protect their savings, and cryptocurrencies like Dash allow them to do this by holding value against the US dollar.

Another area to note is that the richest 10 DASH holders currently hold 10.1% of the total coin value, which is almost double that of Bitcoin and Bitcoin Cash. This could have an impact if one of these major players wanted to influence market movements.

Monero (XMR)

Price at time of writing - $43.22

Available on:

Fiat: Kraken, HitBTC, Bter (CN)

BTC: Poloniex, Bitfinex, Bittrex, Bitsquare

Monero allows users to send and receive funds WITHOUT a public transaction record available on the blockchain. All Monero transactions are private by default. If you believe in privacy first and foremost, then Monero ticks all the boxes. The currency is designed to be fully anonymous and untraceable. This goes as far as their development team, which unlike other coins has no public CEO or figurehead.

Monero also uses "ring signatures", a special type of cryptography to ensure untraceable transactions. This allows users to receive money, without being able to link the address to the sender. This could be looked at as both a positive or negative depending on your viewpoint regarding anonymity. The ring signatures also conceal the transaction amount, in addition to the identity of the buyer and seller. Unlike Dash, Monero has been open source from its inception, so anyone can view the software code for total transparency.

The anonymity of the currency has made it a favorite of the dark web. Before its shutdown, darknet market site AlphaBay had adopted Monero as well as BitCoin to process transactions. Everything from illegal drugs, weaponry and stolen credit cards were traded on the platform. Its anonymity has also made Monero a favorite among ransomware hackers.

It remains to be seen if Monero will branch out to more legitimate use, such as to conceal one's true net worth. Or if it will continue to be the favorite coin of more illicit industries, preventing it from mass adoption versus other coins. This uncertainty could be used to speculator's advantage as they seek to profit from mass adoption potential.

Litecoin (LTC)

Price at time of writing - $40.11

Fiat: Coinbase, Poloniex

BTC: Nearly all exchanges support BTC to LTC transactions

The original altcoin, Litecoin has represented unglamorous yet steady growth in a cryptocurrency scene fueled by hype and large boom/bust cycles. Because of this, many analysts have deemed it the "low risk coin". Announced in 2011 with the intention of being "silver to Bitcoin's gold" and rectifying the shortcomings that Bitcoin faced at the time. Litecoin's coin limit is 4x the amount of Bitcoin's at 84 million coins making it too, a deflationary currency, The time to create a block is 2.5 minutes, a quarter of Bitcoin's 10 minutes.

Litecoin was the long standing second largest cryptocurrency by market capitalization before the rise of Ethereum in 2017.

Litecoin's ability to handle a higher volume of transactions due to its speed of block generation gives it a major advantage over Bitcoin. This means merchants can send and receive payments near instantly with zero transaction costs. Bitcoin on the other hand would take four times as long to process the same transaction at a higher cost. Litecoin also possesses one of the most active development teams in all of cryptocurrency, allowing the coin to undergo regular cutting edge upgrades such as being the first coin to adopt Segregated Witness (SegWit) technology. This also gives the coin the advantage of having the second most secure blockchain after Bitcoin itself.

Another advantage for would be investors is the uptake on major exchanges. Nearly all of the biggest cryptocurrency exchanges support Litecoin purchases in fiat currency including Coinbase in March 2017, which was great news for US and EU investors. In terms of market behavior, generally Bitcoin and Litecoin follow a similar pattern in terms of increases and decreases in the currency value. Many investors choose Litecoin as a supplementary option to Bitcoin in order to diversify their portfolio.

For those interesting in mining, Litecoin's algorithm is far simpler which makes the mining costs and barriers to entry lower. Litecoin runs on the Scrypt algorithm whereas Bitcoin runs on the SHA-256. The main significance of this in practical terms is a lower mining cost as Scrypt is less intensive on Graphic Processing Units (GPUs). In 2017, Bitcoin mining is no longer a viable option for the novice or home based miner, whereas Litecoin mining can still turn a profit, even when factoring in electricity costs in first world countries.

Litecoin's detractors have criticized the coin for being "just another Bitcoin with no innovation". The coin was also the victim of a Chinese pump and dump scheme in 2015 when investors accumulated 22% of all the coins in existence before dumping them.

Factom (FCT)

Price at time of writing - $19.71

Fiat: Coincheck (JP), Yuanbao (CN)

BTC: Poloniex, Bittrex

Like Ethereum, Factom expands on ways to use blockchain technology outside of just currency.

While Ethereum is based on two way verification and ensuring contracts are unbreakable. Factom promises to do the same with large blocks of data by providing a record system that cannot be tampered with. This would allow businesses, governments to provide a track record of data without alteration or loss. The practical applications for this include legal applications, company accounts, medical records and even voting systems. Just imagine a world where it was physically impossible to rig an election, or where an accounting scandal like Enron couldn't happen again.

Like other projects utilizing blockchain, Factom cannot be altered because no single person runs the network. The network is collectively owned by millions of users, independently of each other. While data owned by one person is prone to malevolence, hacking, user error and alteration, the same is not possible with data owned by an entire network.

With regards to investing, like Ether is to Ethereum, Factoids are the "currency" of the Factom system. The more applications that are generated using Factom, the more these Factoids are worth.

Factom has already secured a deal with consulting firm iSoftStone to provide blockchain based administration software projects for cities in China. The deal includes plans for auditing and verification services.

Of the technology, Factom CEO Peter Kirby stated "We believe that this will help developers create a whole new class of accountable and tamper-proof business systems. This could be in insurance, financial services, medical records, or real estate – any system where record keeping is essential."

Like other blockchain technology, common questions surrounding Factom are ones of scalability and wider technology adoption. The other main drawback to Factom investing is whether the team can run the system at a consistent profit going forward - or whether the technology will lead to a race to the bottom in terms of price.

Neo (NEO)

Price at time of writing - $7.89

Available on:

Fiat: Yunbi (CN), Jubi (CN)

BTC: Bittrex, Binance

One of these earliest Chinese based blockchain projects, Neo, formely known as Antshares prides itself on being open source and community driven. The coin has been compared to Ethereum in the sense that it runs smart contracts instead of acting as a simple token like Bitcoin. The project is developed by a Shanghai based company called ONCHAIN.

In a June 2017 press conference held at the Microsoft China HQ in Beijing, the Antshares founder Da Hongfei announced the rebranding to Neo as well as some projects in the pipeline. These included collaborating with certificate authorities in China to map real-world assets using smart contracts.

Neo's base in China allows it unique access to the world's 2nd largest market and the largest cryptocurrency market which could be seen as a unique plus when compared to other cryptocurrencies. However current drawbacks include a limited number of wallets for the coin itself.

At the event - Srikanth Raju, GM, Developer Experience & Evangelism and Chief Evangelist, Greater China Region, Microsoft, said that ONCHAIN is "one of the top 50 startup companies in China." Support and positive press from a global powerhouse like Microsoft can only be a positive for Neo going forward.

Perhaps the biggest determining factor for NEO going forward is support from the Chinese government. While other cryptocurrencies suffer from legal battles with governments, Neo's relationship with the leadership has been low key if somewhat positive, with founder Da Hongfei attending government conferences and seminars on cryptocurrency and blockchain technology.

One thing to be wary of with Neo is once again, a Chinese factor. This time it's the language barrier, as much of the news about the coin is published in Chinese originally, there is significant potential for mistranslations in the English speaking world. For example, "partnerships" with Microsoft and Alibaba (China's largest eCommerce company) have been overstated due to poor translations from Chinese news sources. That doesn't mean collaborations like this aren't possible in the future though.

The smart contracts running on Neo include equities, creditor claims, bills and currencies.

Update as of August 2017: NEO is currently trading at $51.99 - in just a few short weeks a price increased of over 500%

Golem (GNT)

Price at time of writing - $0.26

Available on:

Fiat: Yunbi (CN)

BTC: Poloniex, Bittrex, Liqui

Golen is a coin token, based on Ethereum blockchain technology. Described by some commentators as the "AirBNB of computing", the value of the coin is centered around the software that can be developed using it.

The founders of the Golem Project refer to it as a "supercomputer", with the ability to interconnect with other computers for various purposes. These include scientific research, data analysis and cryptocurrency mining. For example, if your computer has unused power, using the Golem network, you can rent that power (hence the AirBNB comparison) to someone else who needs it. The user who needs the extra power, has the ability to access supercomputer levels of processing power for a fraction of the cost of actually owning the processing power themselves.

The ability for users to earn money for their unused computing power is, in theory, a no-brainer, however what remains to be seen is the practical application of the technology. The Golem team's lack of marketing visibility also appears to hurt the coins value in recent times. The lack of ability to buy GNT using fiat currency (such as USD) is also a drawback for the mass market.

It should be noted that the technology is still very much in the early development stages and as of July 2017, the team are still looking for alpha testers for the project. The Golem Project has a very real possibility of petering out into nothing. On the flip side - there is tremendous potential for large future gains with the price of a coin still under $0.30.

STEEM (STEEM)

Price at time of writing - $1.10

Available on:

Fiat: OpenLedgerDEX (Eur)

BTC: Poloniex, Bittrex

Steem represents one of the more intriguing cryptocurrencies available on the market today. The currency itself is based on the social media platform Steemit. Users can publish content such as blog posts and long form articles, and this content is rewarded in the form of digital currency. Similar to how Reddit users receive upvotes, Steemit users receive Steem tokens known as Steem Dollars. The financial incentive ensures that users strive to produce quality content. The platform allows posts on a multitude of topics ranging from cryptocurrency discussion, to sports news and even poetry.

Steem dollars are worth the equivalent of $1 at the current exchange rate. They must be converted to Steem in order to exchange to fiat currency or other cryptocurrencies. The reasoning behind this is so they can be pegged to the value of the US dollar in order to decrease the risk of inflation devaluing them. Steemit goes further and actually gives users a 10% interest rate on any Steem dollars held in their account for more than a year.

The main drawback is that the success of the coin itself is based on the success of the platform. If the website reaches a plateau in traffic, so will the coin's value. Others have questioned the validity of the site itself, and whether it may be a large scale pump and dump or even a pyramid scheme. The criticism comes from the fact that many of the most upvoted posts were ones that promoted the Steemit platform itself. Concerns have also been raised with automatic posting bots stealing content in order to gain extra voters.

Creators of the site responded to the criticism by saying that there are certain safeguards in place designed to keep content fresh and give users an extra incentive to hold on to their Steem coins. Their way of doing this is with something known as Steem Power. Steem Power is a way for users to lock up their coins in the long run by directly investing them into the platform itself. By converting Steem to Steem Power, users have a greater weighting of upvotes on the platform and essentially become "power users" for lack of a better term.

One advantage Steem possesses versus other cryptocurrencies is that by design it is the easiest currency to access with zero investment. Instead of simply buying coins on an exchange, or spending money on computer hardware needed to mine coins, users can simply sign up on the website for free and begin posting content in order to gain coins. It represents the lowest barrier to entry for any asset in the cryptocurrency market. Although making significant gains may be tough initially, users have made thousands of dollars worth of Steem from just a single post.

IOTA (MIOTA)

Price at time of writing - $0.92

Available on:

Fiat: Bitfinex

BTC: Bitfinex

IOTA, or the rather uninspiringly named Internet of Things (IOT) Coin, is another coin based on blockchain technology, but with a twist.

The team behind IOTA is basing their hopes on a project known as Tangle, which is a technology currently in development that can be described as a blockchain without blocks. In theory, if Tangle does succeed, an entire network can be decentralized. This would lead to ZERO scalability problems that every other coin faces. To be frank, if the technology does indeed work - it could be a complete game changer for the cryptocurrency scene. In more practical terms, imagine a world without unnecessary middlemen, and think of the sheer cost-saving this would achieve.

The underlying theory behind the coin is near-zero transaction costs, even for transfers of minute amounts of money - something that no other coin or technology promises right now - not even giants like Bitcoin or Ethereum. By focusing on these micro, or nano payments, there are countless uses for both consumer and business based financial technology. The technology is open source, so anyone can see the code behind it, and follow along with the coin's development - if you are so inclined.

The reason for the low price of the coin as it currently stands, is that the technology is right now still firmly theoretical. Issues that plague all cryptocurrency technologies like mass adoption and security will have to be resolved before the coin can take the next step. The development team have many issues to overcome in just the construction of the technology, let alone the marketing.

Dogecoin (DOGE)

Price at time of writing - $0.0019

Available on:

Fiat: YoBit, BTC38 (CN)

BTC: HitBTC, Poloniex, Bittrex

A meme that ended up with actual monetary value. Favored by Shiba Inus worldwide, dogecoin was invented by Jackson Palmer in 2013 and became something of a fad in the cryptocurrency world.

Dogecoin's value largely comes from an internet form of "tipping". The most prominent example of this is holders donating Dogecoin to Reddit users for posts they enjoyed. Dogecoin eventually became the second most "tipped" cryptocurrency after Bitcoin and the market for Dogecoin exploded to a peak of $60million market cap in early 2014. A campaign to send the Jamaican bobsled team to the Winter Olympics was funded in part by the coin and $25,000 worth was donated to a UK service dog charity.

The coin flamed out almost as quickly as it rose after Dogecoin backed exchange Moolah filed for bankruptcy and CEO Ryan Kennedy aka Alex Green/Ryan Gentle was sentenced to 11 years in prison on sexual assault charges. Kennedy was estimated to have caused $2-4million dollars worth of losses for those who funded the project.

The coin's present day status remains that of a lighthearted, fun community based project that rewards forum posts. Dogecoin still possess one of the most active communities of any cryptocurrency and supporters hope that one day the coin will return to its position as one of the internet's most tipped coins.

Where to store your cryptocurrency - Wallets & Cold Storage

Once you've successfully bought some cryptocurrency, be it Bitcoin, Ethereum or another altcoin, you'll need somewhere to safely store it.

Your cryptocurrency wallet is akin to a regular fiat currency wallet in the sense that you can use it to store and spend money, in addition to seeing exactly how much money you have. However cryptocurrency wallets differ from fiat currency wallets because of the technology behind how the coins are generated. As a reminder, the way the technology works means your cryptocurrency isn't stored in one central location. It is stored within the blockchain. This means there is a public record of ownership for each coin, and when a transaction occurs, the record is updated.

You can store your cryptocurrency on the exchange where you bought it like Coinbase or Poloniex, it is advisable to not do this for a number of reasons.

1. Like any online entity - these exchanges are vulnerable to hacking, no matter how secure they are - or what security measures they take. This happened with the Mt. Gox exchange in June 2011

2. Your passwords to these exchanges are vulnerable to keyloggers, trojan horses and other computer virus type programs

3. You could accidentally authorize a login from a malicious service like coinbose.com (example) instead of coinbase.com

Cold storage refers to any system that takes your cryptocurrency offline. These include offline paper wallets, physical bearer items like physical bitcoin or a USB drive. We will examine the pros and cons of each one.

Cryptocurrency wallets have two keys. A public one, and a private one. These are represented by long character strings. For example, a public key could be 02a1633cafcc01ebfb6d78e39f687a1f0995c62fc9 5f51ead10a02ee0be551b5dc [4] - or it could be shown as a QR code. Your public key is the address you use to receive cryptocurrency from others. It is perfectly safe to give your public key to anyone. Those who have access to you public key can only deposit money in your account.

On the other hand, your private key is what enables you to send cryptocurrency to others.

---

[4] This is not a real wallet address, do not send money to it

For every transaction, the recipient's public key, and the sender's private key are used.

It is advisable to have an offline backup of your private key in case of hardware failure, or data theft. If anyone has access to your private key, they can withdraw funds from your account, which leads us to the number one rule of cryptocurrency storage.

The number one rule of Cryptocurrency storage: Never give anyone your private key. Ever.

Paper Wallets:

Paper wallets are simply notes of your private key that are written down on paper. They will often feature QR codes so the sender can quickly scan them to send cryptocurrency.

Pros:

- Cheap

- Your private keys are not stored digitally, and are therefore not subject to cyber-attacks or hardware failures.

Cons:

- Loss of paper due to human error

- Paper is fragile and can degrade quickly in certain environments

- Not easy to spend cryptocurrency quickly if necessary - not useful for everyday transactions

Recommendations:

It is recommended you store your paper wallet in a sealed plastic bag to protect against water or damp conditions. If you are holding cryptocurrency for the long-term, store the paper inside a safe.

Ensure you read and understand the step-by-step instructions before printing any paper wallets.

Bitcoin:

http://bitaddress.org

http://bitcoinpaperwallet.com

Ethereum:

http://myetherwallet.com/

Litecoin:

https://liteaddress.org/

For all other currencies - consult a reputable cryptocurrency forum for the latest recommendations on paper and offline storage wallets.

Hardware Wallets

Hardware wallet refer to physical storage items that contain your private key. The most common form of these are encrypted USB sticks.

These wallets use two factor authentication or 2FA to ensure that only the wallet owner can access the data. For example, one factor is the physical USB stick plugged into your computer, and the other would be a 4 digit pin code - much like how you use a debit card to withdraw money from an ATM.

Pros:

- Near impossible to hack - as of the time of writing, there have been ZERO instances of hacked hardware wallets

- Even if your computer is infected with a virus or malware, the wallet cannot be accessed due to 2FA

- The private key never leaves your device or transfers to a computer, so once again, malware or infected computers are not an issue

- Can be carried with you easily if you need to spend your cryptocurrency

- Transactions are easier than with paper wallets

- Can store multiple addresses on one device

- For the gadget lovers among you - they look a lot cooler than a folded piece of paper

Cons:

- More expensive than paper wallets - starting at around $60

- Susceptible to hardware damage, degradation and changes in technology

- Different wallets support different cryptocurrencies

- Trusting the provider to deliver an unused wallet. Using a second hand wallet is a big security breach. Only purchase hardware wallets from official sources.

The most popular of these are the Trezor and Ledger wallets. For altcoins that are not supported by these wallet, you can create your own encrypted USB wallet by following online tutorials.

Cryptocurrency Investing Mindset

FOMO & FUD - 2 Terms to be Cautious of

In cryptocurrency terms, FOMO and FUD are two of the most potentially dangerous words in an investor's lexicon. No, they aren't the latest hotshot coins coming out of China, they are acronyms that have cost naive traders and investors money.

FOMO - Fear Of Missing Out

Fear of missing out causes people to over invest and throw money at coins without proper research or due diligence. If you spend any time on cryptocurrency forums, you will see hundreds of posts from those new to the market asking for tips on which coins to buy. It seems like every day there is a new shiny object that people are hyping up, causing less experienced investors to blindly throw their money at it. This leads to people buying coins at their peak, and then panic selling them when the coin pulls back a few days later.

The important thing to remember is this, you won't be able to win on every investment you make. You won't be able to buy every single coin at the right time, and people will make money where you cannot. The important thing is to only measure yourself against yourself, and take stock of your own profit/loss sheet. Before you invest in a coin, take a second to ask yourself why you are choosing to do so, and re-examine the fundamentals of the coin itself.

Anxiety caused by potentially missing out on huge returns is only natural, and something that nearly all of us suffer from. The best way to combat this is to understand blockchain technology, and to research each coin individually before deciding to invest. By making smart, reasoned investments, you have a much better chance of long term profits.

FUD - Fear, Uncertainty and Doubt

Fear, uncertainty and doubt is information to dissuade investors from believing in cryptocurrencies and their applications. This can be anything from spreading of misinformation (such as the fake Vitalik Buterin death rumors), to news reports discounting real world usage of cryptocurrency technology.

Certain nefarious cryptocurrency figures have used FUD to push their own agenda while attempting to harm the growth of other coins. This is where it is important to differentiate from reasonable criticism and analysis of a coin vs. FUD. The more informed you are, the easier it is for you to see the difference.

Where you are getting your news from is another factor. Social media is the king of FUD, go to any crypto group on Facebook or watch a YouTube video from one of the larger channels and you will see commentors spreading FUD on every video. Instead, focus on larger crypto news websites where FUD is less prevalent, and remember to consume your news from more than one source.

Short term gain vs. Long term investment

Billionaire hedge fund manager and cryptocurrency investor Michael Novogratz made a very good analogy when he compared the current state of the market to the third inning of a baseball game. The market is still very much developing, and there are a number of short and long term events that can effect the price of currencies.

Unlike regular stock market, the cryptocurrency market is running 24/7 365 - there are no delays between information coming to light and the market reacting, there is no dead time.

If you believe in the technology behind the currencies, then these coins absolutely make sense as a long term investment. With many coins, time in the market beats timing the market, which is where our next acronym comes from.

HODL: Hold On (For) Dear Life

A backronym that is a play on "hold" - it focuses on holding on to your coins even when the market is dropping.

A more lighthearted explanation comes from Bitcointalk forum poster "GameKyuubi" who inadvertently invented the term in 2013 while inebriated (author's note: Do not trade or purchase cryptocurrency under the influence)

"WHY AM I HOLDING? I'LL TELL YOU WHY. It's because I'm a bad trader and I KNOW I'M A BAD TRADER.
I SHOULD HAVE SOLD MOMENTS BEFORE EVERY SELL AND BOUGHT MOMENTS BEFORE EVERY BUY BUT YOU KNOW WHAT NOT EVERYBODY IS AS COOL AS YOU."

With any long term investment, you are going to see market downturns - that's simply how capitalism works. If you panic and sell every time you see a slight dip (and with cryptocurrencies, that's going to happen A LOT), then you've got a surefire way to lose money in the long run.

HODL'ing of course has its potential downsides as well, with more and more coins coming to market - it's obvious that not all of them will continue to go up in price. You can compare it to the regular stock market with blue chip stocks and penny stocks. Just because a penny stock or small market cap cryptocurrency is currently trading for $0.08, does not mean it has the right to rise indefinitely. If the company or people behind the cryptocurrency don't fulfill their promises to the market, then the coin's value will crash and it will eventually become obsolete.

Remember - hindsight is easy. Timing market movements in a market as volatile as cryptocurrencies on the other hand, is not. Approach each investment with caution, and proper research.

Paper profits vs. Actual profits

Remember, until you have sold your coins, any profit you have made is strictly on paper. With the cryptocurrency market being as volatile as it is, profit margins drastically shift and can do so on a daily, or even an hourly basis. That is why I recommend taking intermediate profits for yourself when investing, you do this by sell a proportion of your holdings at a profit.

For example, you buy 1 coin at $100, 1 month later the coin's value has risen to $150. If you trade out $75 worth of the coin at $150, then you still have 0.5 coins worth $75 on paper and an extra $75 in cold, hard cash. Taking money for yourself is a smart play, and something you should absolutely do if you are looking to make consistent profits over time.

The inverse rule of this is to not sell on the dip. If you followed rule number one of investing which was to not invest more than you could afford to lose, you have zero reason to sell at a loss. Yes, you may see scary headlines with "Ethereum drops 40%" or "Litecoin is crashing", but in the long-run, the majority of these coins return to their previous, and even higher levels. If you sell at a loss, then your money is gone forever.

The Chaincoin Pump and Dump Scheme - Why You Should Always Research a Coin Before Buying

The following is a lesson in smart investing, and who you get your information from.

Chaincoin (CHC) was a cryptocurrency that underwent a meteoric prise rise from $0.05 to over $6 in under a week. Prior to this, the coin was only available on two small cryptocurrency exchanges and had very little total trading volume. The official Github (programming community) and Twitter accounts had been dead for months prior to this, and very few technical milestones had been accomplished.

Despite this, a YouTube channel known as HighOnCoins started heavily promoting the coin. Videos titled "Buy ChainCoin $CHC" appeared on the channel. The channel also encouraged users to set up masternodes (which required 1000 CHC). The channel encouraged people to buy and hold indefinitely rather than trading out for a profit. The underlying theory behind this was that if everyone invested and held the coin, then the price would continue to increase and grow.

However Chaincoin suffered from many fundamental flaws including:

- Lack of differentiation from other coins

- Lack of innovation from developers

- Zero real world applications versus other coins

The initial surge in investing caused a stir in the cryptocurrency community. Mixed reactions ranging from confusion from investors focused on coin fundamentals, to excitement from uninformed players who believed they were about to get rich quick.

The coin reached an all time high of $6.81 on July 14th 2017, a few days later, developers returned to the coin's GitHub page and made a couple of superficial changes. Within 5 days the price of the coin crashed back to $1. HighOnCoins claimed this was as a result of hackers, although exchange activity showed a large dumping of coins from a few traders.

Chaincoin currently trades at $0.32.

GitHub blog Store of Value summarized the incident with the following statement "This was a blatant transfer of wealth from the foolish to the nefarious." Let this be a lesson, never invest in a coin based on hype. Instead, do so on fundamentals and belief in the technology.

Conclusion

I hope you have learned many things about cryptocurrency and how you can profit from investing or trading in these coins. There are various factors to consider when investing in coins and you can use these to decide on an investing or trading strategy.

You may want to read this material one or two more times, and make some choices as to what your goals are for your relationship with the cryptocurrency market.

Next, decide how you will go about reaching those goals. Decide on a cryptocurrency exchange and how you will store your assets BEFORE investing in any one or more coins.

Then plan out how much you will invest in each coin. Remember, diversity is important and you should never have all of your long-term holdings in a single coin.

If you are going to buy cryptocurrencies, do so using Dollar cost averaging – this means that you don't buy all of your coins in one trade but instead buy a fixed amount every month, week or even day throughout the year. This allows you to not be tied to a single price and instead average out your investments so they are less exposed to volatile price movements.

Trade rationally, not emotionally. If you plan on holding coins for the long-term, do not check charts every few hours, or you will drive yourself crazy. Things change quickly in this market so stay informed on cryptocurrency news and happenings, you can do this in less than 30 minutes per day. Ensure you consume information from a variety of non-biased sources.

And never invest in a coin because "some guy on the internet" told you to.

Finally, if you found this book useful, I would greatly appreciate it if you would review this book on Amazon.

Thank you for reading, I hope you make A LOT of money in the cryptocurrency market.

P.S.

If you sign up for Coinbase using this link, you will receive $10 worth of FREE BITCOIN after your first purchase of more than $100 worth of any cryptocurrency.

http://bit.ly/10dollarbtc

CPSIA information can be obtained
at www.ICGtesting.com
Printed in the USA
BVHW042239200521
607797BV00006B/1361